Through the Flame

Traelea Harper

Presentation by *BookLeaf Publishing*

Web: www.bookleafpub.com

E-mail: info@bookleafpub.com

ISBN: 9789357740265

First edition 2023

ACKNOWLEDGEMENT

To the ones who gave glimpses of hope to me during my journey through the dark, I owe so much thanks and gratitude. Most importantly to my children who have been my grounding force and reasons for taking the next step towards the light. Without all involved there would be no flames of hope.

PREFACE

Is it the beginning of night or the end of one day?
Both answers are right, only your perception can say.

To thrive not survive

The funny thing about being a survivor is that
you make a home in abuse.
It's like you sabotage any chance at kindness and
hang the gift of love with a noose.

Before you were grown, grief ravaged your
spirit.
If there was a mutter of hope, it seemed like you
were the only one to hear it.

Disapproval of who you were took on anger for
your face.
Foreign are the people who operate with
kindness, compassion, encouragement and
gentle grace.

Safety to you looks like pain, and sadness is a
breath of fresh air.
Afterall, your protectors only taught you these
things because "life is hard and never fair".

They built you tough so that not even death
could kill.
Numb to everything is what you became, you
forgot what it's like to feel.

No one wanted a little soul to speak with a wise
voice.
They instilled fear of punishment that left
silence or defense as the only choice.
.

Those shadows I adopted made sure that my
souls call would survive.
I'm grateful that we made it, now let's heal and
finally THRIVE!

Reflection projection

Quit expecting honest advice from people who
can't even look in the mirror.
Being seen for who they are, that is their biggest
fear.

They walk around and tell half truths while
hiding behind the mask.
Keeping up with all their smoke and mirrors
must be quite the task.

They project and gossip on everyone else's
flaws.
Did they mention the fine print in the mirror
mirror clause?

You see people who sit around and clap for
another's demise,
They are the very people who have won that
same exact prize.

It takes one to know one, isn't that what they
say?
Shadows expose the truth so look at it this way...

Until darkness sits with a mirror to do some
self-reflection.
All the things hiding within will be exposed as
outward hurtful projection.

A million and one

5

I've died a million deaths, so really what's one
more?
The gift of death is mediocre at best, always an
opened door.

You want a gift worth receiving that no price tag
can replace?
Then first cut off those shambles and stare death
in the face.

Tell that mother fucker you'll use the hurt, guilt,
and shame
To build a life worth living and an everlasting
name.

Overgrown

Finding all the pieces of you starts with a road
most won't travel.
It's overgrown, not paved, with wash boarded
gravel.

But for a curious mind with a story to be told,
The adventure down this road has secret sights
to behold.

Only the brave rebels take the path deep into the
hollow.
Soon enough you'll only have yourself to listen
to and your heart to follow.

You'll fight the logic that you've used to survive,
But in the journey of this grand discovery you
will learn to thrive.

Some challenges are sent to mold us through
trial.
Don't feed doubt or you'll fall trap to denial.

Temptations will be scattered along the way,
If you realize something is off, definitely don't
stay.

This place holds trickery and plenty of
confusion.
You'll question your entire existence thinking it
was all just an illusion.

Find a spot where you can be silent and still.
Plant some roots, there's plenty of time to kill.

The more you rush, the longer it takes.
Learning patience is part of the stakes.

Ultimately this discovery is one of self worth.
You have so much value to bring to this earth.

Daring to be different is what brought you this
way.
Being the black sheep paid off on the crossroads
that day.

Being unique taught you not to fear the
unknown
Thank the heavens above for the for the travelers
sent down the path that's overgrown.

Redemption

I was no longer just living to die, I had a real
desire to live
I decided to seek out what my soul had to give

Anxiety, depression, lies, lack and fear
No wonder God's voice was so hard to hear

Through all of my trauma I learned how to
poorly cope
Alcohol, sex , self harm, now throw in some
dope.

It's fine right? That's what they all do.
They take one shade of darkness and turn it to
two.

Before I knew it I was the devil's right hand
man.
Death, sadness and destruction, that was the
plan.

But there was one big thing the devil failed to
see.
I wasn't walking alone, God had already laid
claim on me.

In my darkest moments I had my own doubt
"God what are you doing?" He replied "I'm
guiding you out."

Don't think for a second God won't pick the
broken, the lost, and confused.
The soul with riddled in pain, tears, and strife,
flat out abused.

I listened in the stillness to my heart and let my
soul speak.
God's grace found me worthy, so all glory to him
I'll shout from the peak.

From the pits of hell God took me to the highest
mountain above,
"Here's your shot at redemption, sweet girl. Now
go on, love."

Sharp Tongue

My tongue is always hurting from the words
trying to escape.
It's been dealt a living hell and an awful hand at
fate.
A woman with a sharp tongue is a target to
berate.

Don't you dare speak a strong opinion, that
thought alone is outright insane.
Bite that tongue, don't flinch, you can handle the
pain.

Carrying a truth so bold it starts to swell from
words never to be spoken.
Afterall, no good words come from a tongue
who shares a house with a heart in a human
that's broken.

Karmic Debt

A piece of me died with the memory of us that
day .
The life I dreamed of had suddenly slipped
away.

The void in surrender was quite a sight to see.
I had to say goodbye to the me that loved you
and the you that loved me.

The people we are deserve a love Pure and true.
Your karmic debt is paid, now find the one made
for you.

I'm sorry our paths only crossed to fix what was
once shattered.
Maybe the next time around we won't beat each
other's heart until they are battered.

The love that we shared was deep and to the
core
That's the bad thing about lost love, you always
long for more.

Rose-colored glasses

If I am everything and nothing all at the same
time
That means my God is whatever is in that
current sublime.

To dissect all religion could take our forever.
Until we quit dictating another's path, the love
ties are the only things we really sever.

Both the darkness and the light have purpose
and meaning
Too much of the good or the ugly will leave you
lost and feigning.

Since I'm not one thing or the other, I found out
that balance really means,
Everything that makes me, me, falls in the
in-betweens.

I need the me that's gentle and kind AND the me
that's angry and protective.
One doesn't outweigh the other, they are both
important and effective.

The problem comes with limited beliefs because
people don't really know,
"Is this really me or is this the me that's for
society and show."

So you have to have catastrophe that's unique to
the genuine you.
That's when you sit in silence with God in the
deep dark blue.

The very things that break us and kill a part of
our spirit,
Are the things of our unbecoming but our
stubborn minds wouldn't hear it.

God sends us lessons until we find our one
unique soul.
That's when the transformation happens, and we
start becoming whole.

The wounds that seemed so deep we thought
they'd never heal,
Those were the things that taught us just how to
appreciate all we feel.

We felt the sadness of a broken heart.
That's why happiness in the mundane is still a
beautiful form of art.

We felt the anger that turned our vision red.
Now we understand why peace is so pricey, so
we choose to be understanding instead.

We felt the frustration and defeat in the stagnant
rest stage of life.
Now we know the bliss feeling of thriving
doesn't come without some sort of struggle and
strife.

Knowing all of that takes away the me Green
with envy.
It allows me to be exactly me and let you, as you
are, just be.

When we quit looking for differences and put on
the rose-colored glasses of love
Our hearts are filled with genuine gifts sent
straight from OUR God above.

Light the fire

A tear soaked face into the pillow to mask the screams of pain
If I could chose a different fate I'd choose a life that was plain

If you think you want chaos and lessons for the soul
Think twice, being a survivor is no easy role.

When you catch yourself pleading for death call your name
Remember that if you somehow live you'll never be the same

The you that emerges from that hurt is completely new, only fading scars serve as a faint reminder.
Don't forget the time spent fighting like hell praying someone would come help find her.

In the dark alone and aimless with no desire
The girl stood up and saw one way out, so she lit that bitch up in fire.

You first

When people neglect you, walk away
Sacrificing yourself won't make them stay

When you notice their affection suddenly fade
That's when the decision to leave needs to be
made

People who value you won't turn a blind eye to
your requests
If requiring the bare minimum makes you a pest,

Leave those folks right where they are
They are blind to your greatness, don't lower the
bar

Losing yourself in giving to people who are
needy
Speaks volumes on their character, they're
selfish and greedy.

Sure you should help people during your stay
But don't forget to take care of you first, ok ?

Darling

I'm going to tell you the journey to finding the
soul.
It's takes a great leap of faith into a deep dark
hole.

You might question why one would have
discovered this place.
You see they had no options left, they were
staring despair in the face.

After fighting the signs leading to the gold,
Any understanding of direction once known was
robbed or sold.

On the journey to self you'll receive life's
greatest lessons.
It's not punishment for wrong doings but the
cleansing for blessings.

The appreciation of bliss that wonder brings,
Would dwindle if easy access was given to all
precious things.

So shake your head and tell me I'm crazy.

Stop making excuses, just jump but don't plan to
be lazy.

Reaching this point of hardship and defeat,
Might deceive you to believe you have the battle
beat.

I'm here to tell you what I wish I knew,
The war has only begun, it's uoy vs you.

Now look into to the mirror with a gentle gaze.
Surrender your mind and solve the maze.

You'll feel like the free fall is giving you a nice
gentle rest.
Comfort is fleeting stand up and give hell your
best.

You'll see mirror images all over the place.
Which part of you is the real you ? They all have
your face.

This is when you learn the things you once
found funny and attractive,
Were really just your ego spewing defense and
being reactive.

You'll have to search hard and use more than
your sight.

You'll be discouraged and lonely but please don't
give up the fight.

I told you this wouldn't be easy, ya know finding
the way back to the soul.
But you had lose everything to remember you're
already whole.

Now hang up your mentality of lack and
constant fear.
Everyone's soul has a purpose, if you made it
this far your divine abundance is clear.

You did the hard work with nothing more than a
nudge from a knowing.
Now share your light with the world, Darling
you're glowing.

When you think of me

I don't want to be remembered by the value of my dime. When you think of me, just remember "that one time".

You know, the one with memories of you and I. Days filled with hellos before our final goodbye.

Nights filled with laughter and giggles galore Let go of the sadness that cuts to the core.

Remember the hugs, smiles, and love. Together a perfect fit like a hand in a glove.

Don't think of me and only remember the pain. The life we lived wasn't all in vain.

Maybe not today or tomorrow, it's just not yet . I know I'll see you again because the bond we shared two souls can't forget.

So remember me in the good things like the night sky. Let those be what you keep in your heart instead of that "why?

Grow

21

Body, mind, and spirit. Three to one, that's we.
Connected on all sides so God's will lives in Me
.

Led not by sight but blind faith through trust of
destiny.

Finally listening to my heart and following
wherever the wind may go.
I planted God's seed with pure intent and only
one desire, GROW.

Reap the sow

Compassion runs deep in old gentle spirits.
But if you push to far, you'll learn to fear it.

Everything has a direct opposite and when you
mistreat the light you seek.
Lights greatest protector, Shadow, shows up
with havoc to wreak.

So heed my fair warning don't poke the bear.
Karma will serve justice and it's always fair.

You might think you're sneaky and your tactics
quite sly.
But you can't keep secrets from the earth, water,
fire, and sky.

Everything on earth carries it's own spirit.
Connect with your heart and you can see the
message and hear it.

Before you find yourself in the fire being burned
Remember everything you get in this life you
have enevitabley earned

Match compassion with kindness and your
garden will grow.
As the old saying says, you reap what you sew.

Value in the voice

Stop Speaking your truth just to be unheard
Don't waste another syllable of your precious
word

Your record shouldn't be stuck on repeat,
Over and over, giving the same old speech.

Monotony will kill your passion to share.
Never feeling valid will drain your energy, speak
to those who care.

If people don't hear you, they're not yours keep.
Remember your talk is anything but cheap.

If you find yourself surrounded by people who
don't appreciate you,
Let them go, I promise God will send you
someone new.

When you meet the people who are good for
your soul.
You won't have to fight to be heard, and like
embers you will glow.

I know you carry an important message to
deliver.
But don't shoot your arrow too soon make sure
it's complete with its quiver.

Patience will be rewarded with your hearts
greatest desire.
Keep finding your truth, light your voice on fire.

Until people find the value in your voice,
Power through silence is your best choice.

Mirror Mirror

Mirror Mirror who is me?
Who could that reflection be?

I've been asking who am I
I eye am the one most high.

But who is me and who is we?
That's who I want know and see.

If we's purpose is to show life through love.
Grant me the blessings I ask for from above.

Send me connections that can't be broken
The friends I've lost will be the token .

Give me a purpose deep with meaning
This shallow existence has left me feening.

Give me the freedom of time and money
And praise in your name will drip from my lips
like sweet smooth honey

All glory to God for helping me see.
Love is I and I am me.

Trae

27

By the power of three, Let me see.
Who am I supposed to be.

By shedding the darkness I've let in the light.
Show me who I am in plain sight,

I took the torch and let the dark in me burn.
Every bit of this light, I sure did earn.

Now set me free and let me guide.
No longer can this light of mine hide.

Cleansed by fire

Through fire and brimstone from ashes did I
rise.
With impurities cleansed away I was granted
new eyes.

I was no longer living behind the shimmering
veil.
Like all journeys to heaven, I had to start with a
walk in hell.

Facing the monsters that most can't beat,
the hidden gifts passed down from my lineage
made sure evil would suffer defeat.

I was given a purpose of something much
higher.
They say the bigger the shadow, the brighter the
fire.

I put down my fear as a took that life altering
charge at death.
I healed the darkness and light gave me life
through new breath.

The walk in hell is a story all of its own.

In the pits of despair, Unshakeable lessons were shown.

As I take my first steps out of this smokey ash ridden cloud,
I've got a debt to repay by living a life that makes the warrior in me proud.

Sadness to strength

Have you ever been so sad, you can't even cry?
You slowly gave up on living and started
praying to die.

They say they only way out of hell is through.
But I understand why people emerge completely
different and new.

Once the smoke clears and they are no longer
blind.
The persona they carry is gentle and kind.

Some may mistake their tenderness for
weakness.
You shouldn't be fooled, there's a savage hiding
behind that meekness.

They fought to survive in the darkness of night.
Without any promise of what would come out of
this fight.

Led by blind faith and a hope found in their
dreams.
They understand life really isn't as it seems.

Don't mishandle the ones who used the sadness
to emerge from hell.
They were built through struggle and have a
powerful story to tell.

Reflection

I pray after this understanding, lonely and
hopelessness see their way out.
I won't forget their friend, it's a shadow I call,
doubt.

Pain and anger aren't too far behind.
Don't build a home in the shadows and waste too
much time, once it's gone there's no magic
rewind.

Use the lesson you've previously learned,
Time passes rather quickly and more can't be
earned.

You may be eager to watch these shadows fade
out, but please show them respect .
After all you can't forget to remember who gave
you the power to self reflect.

Close the door

The thing bothering me is the need for closure.
I long for something new, I just want to start
over.

Stuck in a fog of envy and self-doubt,
I haven't quite got this grace thing figured out.

It took a long time to build that old version of
me.
But her use is long gone, like a ship lost at sea.

I'm bothered by the haunting knowing that there
is more.
I want the key to a new beginning, so now is the
time I must shut closures door.